S0-DZC-276

Essential Question
How do people figure things out?

Problem Solved

by Frederica Brown
illustrated by Janet McDonnell

Chapter 1

Nothing to Do

"I'm **bored**," Sarah said.

"Me too," Toby said. "There's nothing to do here. Why did we move?"

"You could join a club," Mom said. "You'll make new friends."

"We can't," Sarah said.

"There are no clubs here," Toby said.

"You could start a club," Mom said. "I **imagine** lots of kids would join."

"That's a good idea," Toby said.

STOP AND CHECK

Why did Mom tell Sarah and Toby to start a club?

Toby and Sarah talked to Mike and Heather the next day at school. They were the class presidents. Toby and Sarah **explained** their idea.

Mike and Heather liked the idea. They had a meeting.

"We want to start a club," Toby said. "What would you like to do at the club?"

Everyone had ideas. Mike wanted to play basketball. Heather wanted to skate. Others wanted to watch movies.

Sarah, Toby, Mike, and Heather talked after the meeting. They decided to find a place for the club to meet. They would ask the mayor.

"We need an adult to help," Mike said.

"Mom said she would help," Sarah said.

"We also need an adult to help us run the club," Mike said.

"My dad would help," Heather said.

Homework due Tuesday:
R____ pages 121-126
____even num____

Quiz Wednesday

STOP AND CHECK

What did the meeting show?

7

Chapter 2

Making It Happen

Toby and Sarah asked their mom to help. She set up a meeting with the mayor. Heather's dad found some people to help.

Toby, Sarah, Mike, and Heather started a **petition**. It asked people if they wanted a club.

"We need people to sign the petition," Toby said. "We'll give it to the mayor."

The four children waited outside the school. They asked people to sign their names.

Everyone signed. They thought it was a great idea.

"Good work," Mom said to Toby and Sarah after school. "We're meeting the mayor tomorrow. Bring the petition!"

"We will!" Sarah said.

Toby, Sarah, and their mom went to the mayor's office. The mayor **invited** them in.

Mike and Heather went, too. "We'll be **observers**," Heather said. "We'll tell Dad what happened."

Toby and Sarah's mom explained their idea. The others kept quiet.

STOP AND CHECK

Why did the four children start a petition?

11

"It's a good idea," the mayor said. "We need a club here. There's a building by the basketball courts. It's **perfect** for your club."

"Great!" the children said.

"It needs cleaning up," the mayor said.

"We can do that!" the children said.

"Everyone can help clean the building," their mom said.

Chapter 3

Lots to Do

Everyone got very busy. They planned what to do.

Many people came to help. They had brooms. They had mops.

"Who was the **inventor** of the mop?" Mike grumbled. He picked up a basketball.

"**Bounce** it to me!" Toby said.

"Well, we may have to clean," Sarah said. "But we've solved our problem. We're not bored now!"

STOP AND CHECK

Why were the children no longer bored?

15

Respond to Reading

Summarize

Summarize *Problem Solved.* Use details from the text. Your chart may help you.

Details

↓

Point of View

Text Evidence

1. Reread page 13. How did the children feel about cleaning up the building? Point of View

2. Find the word *sign* on page 9. What does it mean? What clues help you figure it out? Vocabulary

3. How did the characters in *Problem Solved* feel at the beginning of the story? How did they feel at the end? Write About Reading

Compare Texts
Read how Bradley solves the problem of being bored.

Rainy Day

I looked out the window.
The rain came down.
I looked out the window.
My face had a frown.

I was bored.
I was behaving badly.
My dad said, "Bradley,
Find something to do!"

He said, "Watch TV
Or play cards with me!"
But I was bored.
I was behaving badly.
There was nothing
I wanted to do.

Then it was clear.
I had an idea.
I had a thought.
I'd make a fort!

Blankets and boxes,
Bedclothes and baskets,
Cushions and chairs,
All stacked by the stairs.

The fort was ready.

The walls stood steady.

I'm safe inside,

Safe as a soldier

With Dad by my side.

Make Connections

What was Bradley's problem in *Rainy Day*? How did he solve it?

Essential Question

How is Bradley like the characters in *Problem Solved*? Text to Text

Focus on
Literary Elements

Rhyme Poems often use *rhyme* and *alliteration*. Rhyme is when a similar sound is repeated at the end of two or more words. An example of rhyme is, *We'll meet <u>you</u>, At the <u>zoo</u>.* Alliteration is when a consonant is repeated at the beginning of two or more words that are near each other. An example is *a <u>w</u>et, <u>w</u>indy, and <u>w</u>ild day.*

Read and Find The poem *Rainy Day* is written in rhyme. Find the rhymes. Find an example of alliteration.

Your Turn

Work with a partner. Think of examples of alliteration to go with these words: *dog, baby, water.*